97

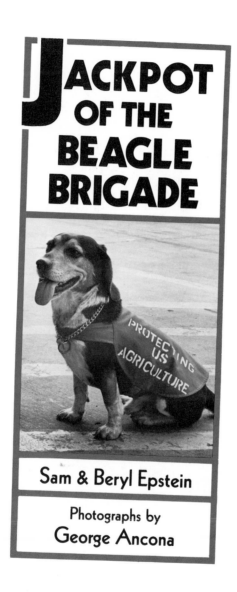

JACKPOT OF THE BEAGLE BRIGADE

PROTECTING US AGRICULTURE

Sam & Beryl Epstein

Photographs by
George Ancona

MACMILLAN
PUBLISHING COMPANY
NEW YORK

Macmillan Publishing Company
866 Third Avenue, New York, NY 10022
Collier Macmillan Canada, Inc.

First Edition
Printed in the United States of America
10 9 8 7 6 5 4 3 2 1

The text of this book is set in 13 pt. Baskerville.
The black-and-white photographs are reproduced in halftone.

Library of Congress Cataloging-in-Publication Data
Epstein, Sam, date.
    Jackpot of the beagle brigade.
    Summary: A photo essay presenting a beagle at work at Kennedy Air-
port sniffing out contraband fruits and meats that many travelers bring
into the country.
    1. Jackpot (Dog)—Juvenile literature. 2. United States. Animal and
Plant Health Inspection Service—Officials and employees—Biography—Juvenile literature. 3. Beagles (Dogs)—Biography—Juvenile literature. 4. Dogs—New York (N.Y.)—Biography—Juvenile literature.
5. John F. Kennedy International Airport—Juvenile literature. 6. Air
lines—Baggage—Inspection—Juvenile literature. [1. Jackpot (Dogs) 2.
Beagles (Dogs) 3. Dogs. 4. United States. Animal and Plant Health
Inspection Service—Officials and employees] I. Epstein, Beryl Wil-
liams, date. II. Ancona, George, ill. III. Title. IV. Title Beagle brigade.
SB981.E67 1987   364.1'42   86-23827
ISBN 0-02-733510-0

TO THE KRENTS
Pam, Ed, Adam,
and Heather

– G.A.

Did you ever know a dog that worked for the United States government? That's what this little brown and white beagle does. His name is Jackpot.

Jackpot works at John F. Kennedy International Airport in New York City. And when he is on the job, he wears the green coat that is his uniform. White letters on one side of the coat tell the name of the government department Jackpot works for: U.S. AGRICULTURE. White letters on the other side tell what Jackpot's job is: PROTECTING U.S. AGRICULTURE. Jackpot helps protect our agriculture—all the farms in our country—by using his nose.

Like most dogs, Jackpot can smell much better than people can. We can smell a sliced onion. But suppose someone put a whole onion inside a plastic bag and then put that bag inside a suitcase and covered it with clothes. Could we still smell it? Jackpot can. He can smell all sorts of vegetables, and seeds and nuts and fruits and meats, too, no matter how well covered they are.

People coming here from a foreign country sometimes bring such foods in their luggage. If those foods came from unhealthy plants or animals, they could spread diseases to American farms. That's why a law says travelers can't bring them into this country. And if luggage inspectors find them in travelers' bags, they take them out and have them burned.

But the inspectors are often too busy to search every corner of every bag. They might miss oranges wrapped in a sweater or a sausage hidden in a shoe. Jackpot helps by letting them know he smells food in a traveler's luggage.

Of course, Jackpot can't talk to the inspectors. But he can give his partner a signal that says, "There's food in here!"

Jackpot's partner is a man named Hal Fingerman. The badge on Hal's shirt tells people he also works for the Department of Agriculture.

Jackpot and Hal start their day's work in Hal's office at the airport. For Jackpot it really begins when Hal picks up his leash and says, "Let's go."

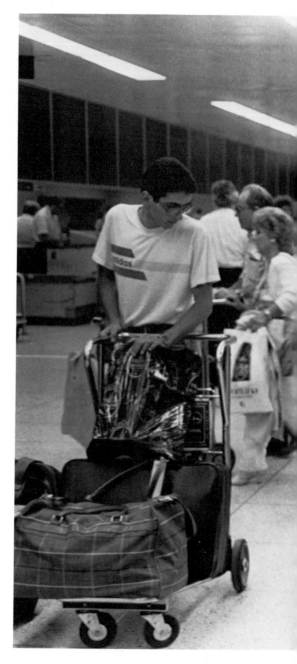

Together they walk out into a big hall. It is filled with people who have just arrived from a foreign country. They are standing beside their piles of suitcases, bags, and packages. They are waiting to take their turns at the long tables where their luggage will be inspected.

Jackpot stops and sniffs at the first pile of luggage he comes to.

When Jackpot finishes sniffing that pile, he moves on to the next one, and then the next.

People smile at Jackpot. "Look at the little beagle!" they say. "Isn't he cute!" A man stoops to scratch his chin. A little girl pats him, and Jackpot wags his tail.

Jackpot comes to a cart piled with suitcases. He starts to sniff around it.

"Keep your dog away from my stuff!" the man says.

"He's just doing his job," Hal replies.

Then Jackpot sits down beside the cart. This is the signal. Jackpot is letting Hal know he has smelled food in the man's luggage.

Jackpot looks up at his partner.

Hal reaches into a pouch hanging from his belt and takes out a dog biscuit. He drops it at Jackpot's feet. Jackpot snaps up his reward.

"Is there any food in your luggage?" Hal asks the man.

"No," the man says. He hands Hal a piece of paper. "Look at my declaration."

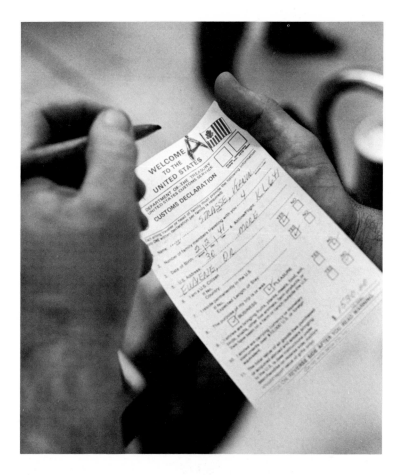

Declarations are forms on which travelers write down the things they got in a foreign country and are bringing into the United States. They must show these forms to the luggage inspectors.

Hal sees that no food is listed on the declaration. But some travelers hide food in their luggage and don't list it. They hope the busy inspectors will not find it.

Hal uses a green pencil to draw an *A* on the man's form. Then he hands it back. "Thank you," Hal says. And he and Jackpot move on.

The green *A* is another signal. It tells the inspector to search that luggage very carefully.

Jackpot sniffs at another pile of luggage. Then he comes to the next one. A woman and two boys are standing beside it. They watch Jackpot sniff all around their bags. They smile at him.

Jackpot sits down. Hal gives him his biscuit.

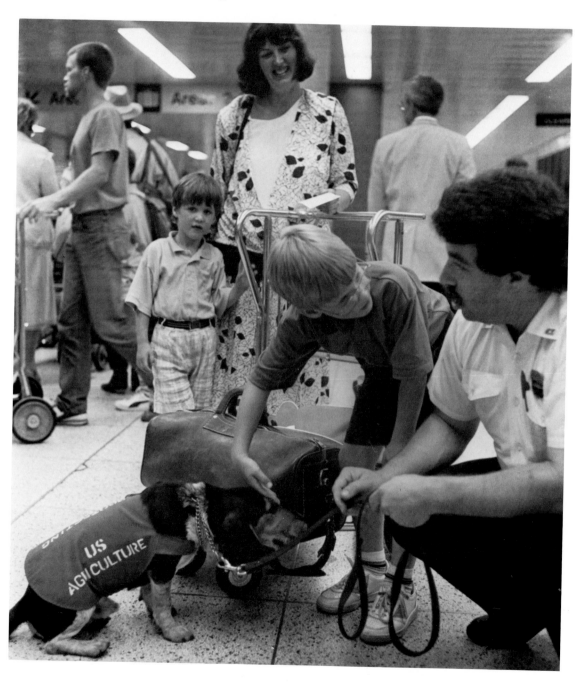

The woman looks at Jackpot's uniform. "How does he protect our agriculture?" she asks Hal. "Or does he wear that coat just because it's so cute?"

"He's protecting our agriculture right now," Hal says. "By sitting down beside your luggage, he's telling me he smells food in it. The inspector may have to take your food away."

One of the boys says, "But my grandmother made cookies and candy just for us!"

"Don't worry," Hal says. "It's all right to have candy and cookies in your luggage. Jackpot is sitting down because he smells some other kind of food."

Then Hal tells the woman about the law against bringing in certain other foods. He asks for her declaration.

"Oh, dear!" the woman says, giving him the form. "We do have some of those foods: some lemons from my mother's tree and one of her homemade sausages. I didn't know we had to list foods, and I didn't know about the law. But I certainly understand it. Will I have to pay a fine?"

"Not if you tell the inspector right away about the food you have," Hal says. He draws a green *A* on her declaration and returns it to her. Then he tugs at Jackpot's leash to let the beagle know they can move on.

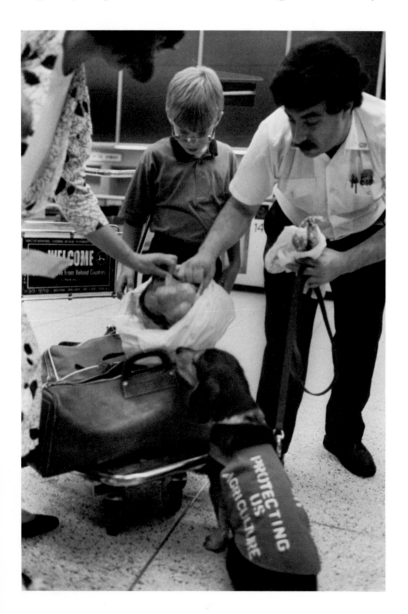

Jackpot sniffs around more luggage piles. He is trotting toward the next one when Hal stops him. Hal sees the man who had not wanted Jackpot to smell his luggage. The man is now standing at one of the long tables. On it is an open suitcase. Behind the table is an inspector.

The inspector nods. The man closes his suitcase. He looks very angry as he walks away with his luggage. The foods Jackpot had smelled in his suitcase have been left behind on the table.

ELEMENTARY SCHOOL LIBRARY
ITHACA, NEW YORK

Jackpot and his partner go on their way through the crowded hall. At each pile of luggage Jackpot stops to sniff. Soon he earns another dog biscuit. And then another. And another.

Jackpot trots up to a tall duffle bag. It is so tall that he has to stand on his hind legs to sniff at the pocket at the top. Jackpot's nose moves all over that pocket. Then his front feet plop to the floor and he sits down. Hal gives him his biscuit.

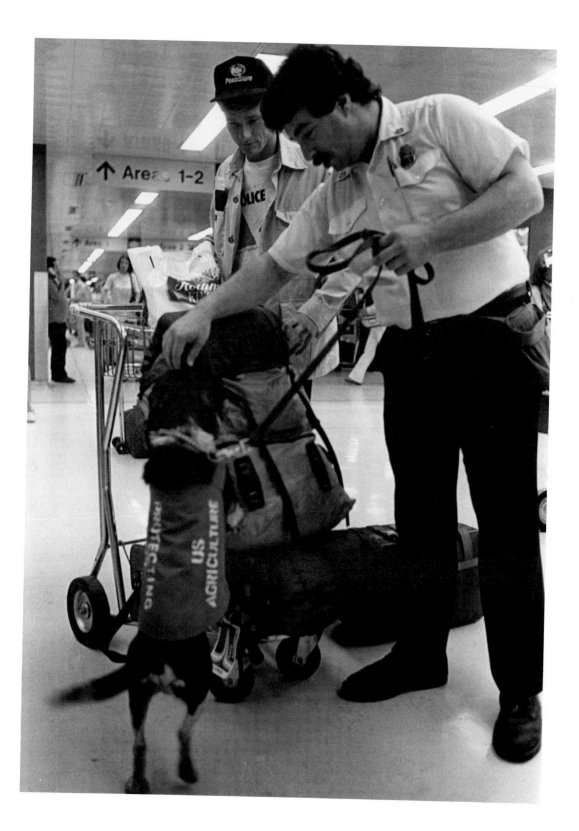

The young man standing beside the duffle bag has been watching Jackpot and grinning. Now he bends down and scratches Jackpot's head. "I've got a dog just like you at home," he says. "I guess you found his smell."

"No," Hal says. "He smelled a food smell in that top pocket."

"But there's no food in there!" the young man says. Then he looks at Jackpot's uniform and at the badge on Hal's shirt. "I get it!" he says. "The dog is a food detective, and you think I'm trying to sneak illegal food into the country. Here—see for yourself."

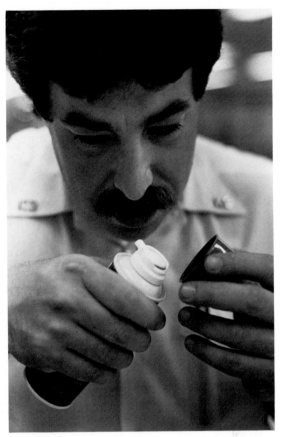

The young man opens the pocket and takes out several objects, one at a time. "What did I tell you?" he says. "Nothing but toothbrush, toothpaste, razor, leaky spray can of shaving cream."

"That shaving cream smells of lime, doesn't it?" Hal says.

"That's right," the young man says.

Then he looks at Hal. They both look at Jackpot. They both smile.

"I told you he smelled a food smell in there," Hal says. "To Jackpot the smell of limes means real limes, not just shaving cream."

The young man laughs. "The next time I land at Kennedy, I'll make sure I have shaving cream that has no smell. Or I'll land at some other airport."

"You'll probably have the same trouble," Hal tells him. "Jackpot was one of the first beagles trained to do this job, but now there are beagles sniffing for hidden foods at other airports, too. We call them the Beagle Brigade."

By now hundreds of travelers have left the airport and gone on their way. The big hall is nearly empty. But in the room where the illegal food is kept before it is burned, the table is piled high!

Hal takes Jackpot to his office for a rest. Jackpot curls up in his own basket beside Hal's desk.

An hour later, when another plane has landed and the big hall is filled again, Jackpot and his partner go back on the job.

It is after eight P.M. when they finally leave the airport. Jackpot rides in his cage in Hal's station wagon.

At Hal's house, Jackpot eats a good dinner. Then he settles down for the night in his kennel in the backyard.

In the morning Jackpot has time to run up and down the yard. He swallows the vitamins Hal gives him.

Jackpot stands quietly while Hal puts toothpaste on a brush and brushes Jackpot's teeth and tongue. Then he lets Hal brush him until his fur is clean and smooth and shiny.

They drive back to the airport. There, in the office, Hal puts fresh dog biscuits in his pouch. He buckles on Jackpot's uniform.

And then Jackpot and his partner go out into
the big hall for another day's work.